DANIEL SANTIAGOE

60 CURRY RECIPES IN THEIR ORIGINAL STYLE

CONTENTS

PREFACE BY AUTHOR

WITH much thankfulness to Mr. A. Egmont Hake for his kindness in writing a preface for my first book on Curries, and great credit is due to *Saturday Review* and humble respect is due to my two masters, Shand, Haldane & Co., of London, who brought me over to England and Scotland, with four other servants, and allowed me to publish a little book to make my desired little fortune, which is highly creditable. From the first edition of 500 copies I fully sold 400, and another hundred copies presented to friends in England and Ceylon. My intention in publishing this second edition is that I have given too little recipes and information in my first book for sixpence each copy. Though I thought it is worth making it an enlarged and revised edition for same price this time, I should like to give good many recipes for making a Curry, and give the names of all Meat and Vegetable in English and Tamil. In each heading of Curries two sorts of ingredients are given—one to be procured in England, the other in Ceylon; and also each Curry will be properly instructed. I have tasted the Curries made by Bengalee, etc., on board of steamers and on shore. They use proper Curry Stuffs, etc., but they flavour it too much; using plenty of ghee and fat mutton, etc.,—these spoil the taste. Just the same with Bombay Curries, but in Madras is the only place you could taste a proper Curry, and also in Ceylon, as a good many cooks of Madras Presidency came to Ceylon several years ago and spread out the art of general cooking in Ceylon. I believe at first the cooking business was instructed by European cooks. At present there is too many cooks in Ceylon; almost every butler, appoo, second servant, kitchen mate, groom, etc., knows to cook a English dinner!!!

Now we shall go on with our Curry business. I recommend to try Curry Powders from several grocers. The best Curry Powder is made of coriander seed (which could be got from the chemist's), saffron, dry chillies, cumin seed, few mustard seed, few pepper corns. If the Curry Powder contains all the above, it is a good Curry Powder. Some Curry Powders tastes of acid, flour, and other mixtures, which I believe is unwholesome in every means. The Tamils use tamarind for the acid taste. To every brown Curries the Singalese use Gorakka (a sour fruit), slightly dried, and lime juice to their yellow Curries. There is much different taste between a Singalese Curry and a Tamil Curry—the taste just differs the same as a Madras beef Curry, No. 4, and a potato Curry (vegetable). The Curries should be treated same as a ordinary entree. If one article you had too much, it will spoil the whole Curry. If the meat over done, no taste in it. If you have all Curry stuffs, etc., at hand, could make a Curry Sauce in ten minutes the longest, and can warm up any meat for table in it (I mean the brown). The white Curry Sauce is not suitable, unless for a vegetable or fish.

I could give several other recipes to Curries, but the above said sixty will be quite sufficient. If you carefully tried the above said Curries will be found most economical.

A Madras woman can beat any other Indian woman in Curry cooking. In several gentry's houses in Madras, etc., they keep a woman to make Curries and prepare vegetables for table—we call her "Thanney Kareyitchi"—besides the cook and kitchen matey.

The Madras Curry always the best, much different than a Bengal or Bombay Curry, to my opinion.

D. SANTIAGOE.

60 CURRY RECIPES IN THEIR ORIGINAL STYLE

No. 1.—HOME-MADE CURRY POWDER.

IN ENGLAND.

- 1 lb. Coriander Seed.
- ½ oz. Saffron.
- 1 Eggspoon Cumin Seed.
- ½ doz. Pepper Corns.
- Small bit of Cinnamon (1 in. square).
- 8 Dried Chillies Capsicums.
- 4 Tablespoons good Rice.

IN CEYLON.

- Coriander.
- Saffron and Cumin Seed.
- Pepper Corns. Cinnamon.
- Dried Chillies—Rice.
- Curry Leaves, and few other things of which cannot be procured in England.

N.B.—I only mention this home-made Curry Powder, if you can procure the above said Curry Stuffs separately from the chemists or grocers. As I heard from a gentleman in Liverpool, "Everything the world produces can be bought in London"!!!

Mode.—Place a frying-pan (not an enamelled one) on fire; soon as it gets hot put in the coriander; when nice and gold colour take it off and put on a plate again. Set the frying-pan on fire and add the cumin seed, pepper corns, dry chillies. Just give a shake, and take it off and give it two or three more shakes and put on a plate, but don't put the saffron in the frying-pan. Now wipe the frying-pan, and set on fire again; when hot, put in the rice, and keep on shaking till each grain gets goldish brown; do not let it burn. The rice on board of ships will answer to this better than you buying from your grocer's; but in the scarcity of above any rice will do.

Now when all these are done we shall have to grind it to a smooth powder. These cannot be done unless you have a stone-made pounder or Curry stone and grinder. The latter I have not seen in England, still there is the finest strong metal stones in England. The Curry stone and grinder is bought for no money in up country of Ceylon, but in Colombo, the chief city here, we pay 50 cents, to Rs. 2 50 cts. each. Curry stone and grinder will last for generations. It is better to grind all Curry stuffs separately and keep each in its own bottle, then you will be careful of what you are about, and you will know how much you are using of each stuff.

For any meat Curry (per lb.) add one table-spoon coriander seed, a saltspoon of saffron, a pinch of cumin seed, dash of pepper, small bit of cinnamon, one-half tablespoon of rice powder; if preferred hot, add a bit

14

of cayenne. For white Curries, only one-half teaspoon of saffron to be added. If at hand, just cut a young capsicum in quarters and add to the Curry. You can add a green chillies to Meat Curries also. If the above home made Curry Powder cannot be done, you shall have to buy three sorts of Curry Powder. Coriander, rice, cumin seed, and pepper (one mixture); cayenne and saffron each separately bottled. Other things can be got from your respective grocers. If you buy a mixed Curry Powder or Paste, it will taste everything too much, as following:—Heat! hot? bitter, sour flour, spice, and too much of yellow colour of saffron, and too much of a nice Curry smell. The fact is, I have tasted several Curry Powders and Paste in England, and also in Scotland, but nothing equal to separate Curry stuffs. If the Curry stuffs, etc., are imported from India to Europe it will keep good for a long time, and will have a good market, except the dry chillies, because there is plenty of cayenne in England. Garlic ginger (green), used for any Meat Curry, it is very healthy and helps to digest the Curry and rice sooner, as parties think Curries are not easily digestible. The Curries must not be prepared too rich, as richness takes away all flavour, and the meat will taste like stewed Curry. The butter you add to fry the Curry stuffs will be quite sufficient to richen the Curry without using fat meat.

No. 2.—BEEF CURRY (Plain).

* 1 lb. Beef (Fresh or Cooked Meat will do).
* 1 Tablespoon Curry Powder (not hot).
* 1 Pint good Milk or strong (Beef) Gravy.
* 1 Large Onion or few small ones.

- 1 Young Capsicum and 1 Tablespoon Rice Powder.
- Small piece of Cinnamon.
- Pinch of Cumin Powder; Salt to taste.

N.B.—In Ceylon we use Cocoanut Milk (the juice), Curry Leaves, and some other Leaves for Spices.

Mode.—Cut the meat in half-inch squares; put into a clean stew-pan, then slice the onions, and add the onions, Curry stuffs, chillies, cinnamon, milk, cumin seed, etc., and salt. Mix all well together, and set on fire for 15 to 20 minutes; do not let it burn. When serving add a few drops of lemon juice. If required hot add a pinch of cayenne when preparing.

No. 3.—BEEF CURRY (Ceylon).

FOR A POUND OF GOOD BEEF (I mean lean).

- 1 Tablespoon Coriander Powder and 1 of Rice Powder.
- ½ Eggspoon Saffron Powder and Pinch of Cumin Powder.
- 1 Pint good Milk or Gravy.
- 1 Large Onion or few small ones.
- 2 Young green Chillies (Capsicum).
- A bit of Cinnamon (if you like spices); Salt to taste.

N.B.—In Ceylon all the Curry stuffs are freshly grinded. Cocoanut Juice, Curry Leaves, etc., are used. This is a very delicious Curry to eat with rice boiled or bread toasted.

Mode.—Cut the meat in half-inch squares and put into a clean stew-pan with the onions sliced, the chillies in quarters; then add all the Curry Powder, etc. Mix well with a wooden spoon and add three parts of a pint of milk or gravy; then salt to taste. Set on slow fire for 15 to 20 minutes; soon as the meat is tender (but not overdone), then add the other quarter of milk and a few drops of lemon juice. Just heat it again and send to table in a vegetable dish with boiled rice separate. If you add gravy to this Curry then you must put in two tablespoons of cream before sending to table.

No. 4.—BEEF CURRY (Madras).

FOR A POUND OF BEEF.

- 2 Tablespoons Coriander Powder and 1 of Rice Powder.
- 1 Saltspoon Saffron and a Pinch of Cumin Powder and Fenugreek.[4]
- ½ Pint of Milk or good Gravy.
- 1 Large or few small Onions.
- A bit of Cinnamon, 2 Cloves (if you wish spices).
- ½ Teaspoon Green Ginger chopped up fine.
- A Small Garlic chopped up fine.
- 1 Large Spoonful of Butter (fresh); Salt to taste.

N.B.—This Curry is made in Madras with or without Cocoanut, but little Tamarind will flavour this Curry better than Lemon Juice. Vinegar, Curry Leaves, etc., are used in Madras and Ceylon. This is a first-class Curry if carefully prepared.

Mode.—Have the meat ready cut in half-inch squares; then slice the onions; put a good stew-pan on the fire, add the butter; soon as the butter gets hot put in the onions and Curry Powder, but not the ginger, garlic, and spices. When the onions, Curry stuffs, etc., are nicely browned, add the meat, garlic, ginger, spices, and give it a turn. Let it stand for a few seconds, then add the milk or gravy, salt, etc.; set on slow fire for about 20 minutes. When sending to table add a few drops of lemon or good pickle vinegar, but tamarind is best. Add little cayenne if preferred hot; a hot Curry is considered always nice and healthy, the cayenne to be added when preparing.

No. 5.—BEEF CURRY (Kabob or Cavap Curry).

- 1½ lb. Lean Beef.
- 2 Tablespoons Coriander Powder and 1 of Rice Powder.
- 1½ Saltspoon Saffron and a good Pinch of Cumin Powder.
- 1 Good Pint of fresh Milk or Gravy.
- 1 Large Onion or few small ones.
- Ginger, about 2 inches long.
- 2 Long Budded Garlics.
- 1 Large Spoon Butter (fresh).
- Spices; Salt to taste.

N.B.—This Curry same as Madras Curry, No. 4, but the meat ought to be of tender part. Must not overdo it, neither burn it. If tamarind used, it is nicer.

Mode.—This is a first-class Curry if carefully prepared. Cut the meat in half-inch squares; the ginger as round as a threepenny piece, and the garlic the same size, but thicker. Now sharpen few thin sticks with points to stick the meat (I mean as large as champagne bottle wire, three to four inches long). Now begin the job; stick one of meat, another of garlic, another of meat, and one of ginger (I mean a piece of meat must be between garlic and ginger). Proceed as above till you finish the meat, etc.; now place a stew-pan on fire; put in the butter and the onions sliced. When nicely browned add the Curry stuffs and the meat. Now let the whole fry gently in the butter for five minutes; now pour the milk in and let it simmer gently for 20 minutes. When serving add a spoonful of cream and a few drops of lemon, and send to table with boiled rice (separate).

No. 6.—BEEF CURRY (Dry).

Same ingredients as for Madras Curry, No. 4, and prepare the same way, but do not add any milk. Add about four tablespoons of good gravy when preparing, but add two tablespoons of cream five minutes before serving. (If I say dry, not very dry, but second to it; add few drops of lemon when sending to table.) This Curry must be put on very slow fire, a hot oven will do; if so, you must look every five minutes in case it burns. This Curry can be eaten with rice, boiled potatoes, or toast if wished. Some dry Curries are done in a frying-pan within ten minutes, only the onions and Curry stuffs should be browned, and the meat mixed with it.

N.B.—Must use a wooden spoon to all Curries when browning the Onion and Curry Stuffs, etc.; better than a plated one.

No. 7.—BEEF CURRY (Ball).

Take a pound of beef free from skin, bone, etc., put into a sausage machine, and get it mashed up; put on a plate, pepper it slightly. Now take ingredients same as for No. 4, and chop fine the ginger, garlic, and mix with the meat with little salt. Now make this meat into balls as large as a marble, flour it, and fry in lard to a brown colour. Do not let it break. Now keep this to a side, and place a good stew-pan on fire, and put in the butter and the onions sliced, and the Curry Powder. When all these nice and brown add the meat balls to it. Just mix slowly, not to break the meat balls. Now add half-pint of good milk, or gravy, and let it stand on a slow fire till wanted. When serving, add a spoonful of cream, few drops of lemon, and salt to taste, and send to table with boiled rice, etc.

N.B.—This Curry must not overdo, neither must the meat be overdone when frying; and when passing the meat through sausage machine, at the same time you can add the spice, garlic, ginger, with the meat to be mashed up. If preferred hot, add little cayenne pepper.

No. 8.—CHICKEN CURRY.

- One good-sized Chicken (about a pound or more).

Other ingredients same as for Madras Curry, No. 4. Now cut up the chicken in half of each joint. Keep it to a side. Now fry the onions, sliced, in a stew-pan, with a large spoon of butter. When the onions are nice and brown, just fry the chicken in it less than half done. Take it out and keep to a side. Now fry the Curry Powder till it is nice and dark brown, then add the chicken, more onions, and other things into the frying Curry Powder, etc., and add half-pint of good gravy, and set it on a slow fire for 20 minutes. When serving, add two large spoons of cream. If it is very dry, add little more gravy to it. A few drops of lemon will flavour it, but I recommend to make the chicken into a "moley," as No. 29. Much nicer to be eaten with rice or treated as an ordinary entree, and the curried fowl (whole) nicer as a joint.

No. 9.—SNIPE CURRY.

Dress four snipes as for serving on toast; then cut in halves, pepper and salt it, roll it in little (or sprinkle with) flour, and fry it in a large spoon of butter or lard, quarter done or nearly half done. Keep it to a side. Now take a good stew-pan, put on fire, melt a spoonful of butter, and fry a large onion, sliced; put in

- 1 Tablespoon Coriander.
- 1 Dessertspoon Rice Powder.
- A pinch of Cumin Powder.
- A pinch of Saffron and Spices.

Let all these fry gently in the butter, then add half-pint of good gravy, salt to taste, and let this stand on a hot oven, simmering gently till required. Five minutes before serving, add the fried *snipes*, with a few drops of lemon juice, and send to table. Do not let it be too juicy, but the half-pint of gravy should be reduced to a quarter-pint. Cayenne pepper should be added if preferred hot Curries. Snipe should only be heated through, and not quite *over*done. This Curry nice with rice, toast, etc. etc. Can almost be treated as an entree.

No. 10.—PIGEON CURRY.

Take four young pigeons and dress same as for salmi of pigeon, and treat the same way as for Snipe Curry, No. 9. Any curry may be made of different taste by reducing the ingredients or exceeding it, or by using tamarind or pickle vinegar instead of lemon juice, or using milk instead of gravy; and to some Curries add cream, and other Curries using cocoanut juice (milk).

No. 11.—PORK CURRY.

One pound of fresh and lean pork, and the ingredients same as for Madras Curry, No. 4; use only three parts of everything. A pinch of Cayenne will flavour this Curry. Tamarind (an acid?) is nicer than lemon juice, vinegar, etc. To use the tamarind, take a piece the size of a large walnut, put into a cup and add about two tablespoons of cold water, and squeeze it with a spoon or with your finger, strain through a clean muslin and add to the Curry. Tamarind is always good for any sort of brown Curry, and lemon juice for yellow or white Curries, and vinegar for "moley," because it is an entree, and not much Curry stuffs are used.

No. 12.—VEAL CURRY.

Everything same as Madras Curry, No. 4, but veal Curry, not nicer. If you have veal chops, treat same as Curried mutton chops, No. 17.

No. 13.—MUTTON CURRY.

FOR ONE POUND MUTTON (WITHOUT FAT).

Ingredients same as for Madras Curry, No. 4 but not the quantity. Only three parts should be taken of each; the Curry stuffs need not be fried as for Madras Curries, but cut the mutton in half-inch squares, put into a stew-pan, and then add the Curry stuffs (powders?), spices, etc., and add a tablespoon of cream when serving, as well as a few drops lemon juice. Curries made from mutton are not so nice as if made from tender part of beef, but in India and Ceylon several castes do not touch beef—they call themselves high caste people, and bear numerous names—they always eat mutton, fowl, vegetable, etc. The Brahman caste never eat any meat of any sort; still they eat the pure juice of beef—as milk, ghee, butter, and another kind of medicine made out of the flesh of the ox, called in Tamil "paroong kayam."

No. 14.—PARTRIDGE CURRY.

I have nothing to say for this Curry, because you can imitate the pigeon Curry; anyhow you must put in strong gravy, as partridge does not taste nice if curried. If you have any partridge left from dinner, the next day you may Curry it same as pigeon, but don't let it simmer too long over the oven. Any kind of game (birds?) can be made same as the pigeon.

No. 15.—TRIPE CURRY.

Take about two lbs. of good, thick part of the tripe, cut them in about four inches square, or not at all, dip it in hot water, not boiling, but nearly so. Then take out and scrape off all the black stuff, and clean it as white as a white tablecloth, and boil it tender as you boil for "Tripe Fricassee." When cool cut it in half-inch squares, slightly pepper it. Place a stew-pan on fire, and put in a lump of butter. When hot add the tripe, fry it to a brownish gold colour, then take out and put in a plate till required. Now add the Curry stuffs, as No. 4, into the stew-pan on the fire, and turn it over and over till nice and brown. Now add the tripe you fried, and half-pint of good gravy, and let it simmer gently on slow fire. When serving add a tablespoon of cream and few drops of lemon. Some nice spices and a pinch of cayenne pepper should be added when frying the Curry Powders. This is a very nice Curry. By-the-by, the gravy you boil the tripe in should be boiled with other bones, vegetables, etc., and add to the Curry instead of other gravy.

No. 16.—LIVER CURRY, WITH BACON.

Take a pound of liver and a piece of fat of bacon, boil both in one pan for quarter of an hour, then take it off the fire, let it cool, then cut it in half-inch squares, add about ¼ lb. bacon to a pound of liver, and treat it same as Madras Curry, No. 4. The Liver Curry considered not nicer. Parties in India and Ceylon (Europeans) do not care much for Liver Curry but as an entree, "Liver and Bacon." A breakfast dish in India and Ceylon.

No. 17.—CHOPS CURRIED.

This is a changeable way to have mutton chops done for breakfast or as an entree for dinner. Take eight good chops, and flavour it the usual as for serving itself (I mean place the chops on a flat dish, pepper and salt it). Vinegar, a dash of Lucca oil, and few drops of sauce, and let these soak for a few minutes, then place a frying-pan on fire, add a lump of butter. When melted add the chops, and fry it in usual way of mutton chops. When done take it off the frying-pan, keep it in a plate. Now take a large onion and slice it, and fry it to a gold colour in the frying-pan you fried the chops, then add all the Curry stuffs to it as said in the Madras Curry, No. 4, except the cayenne, ginger, and garlic. When all these are nicely fried add four spoons of good stock (brown), and now add the chops into the frying-pan. Let it warm, then serve on a hot dish, and send to table with potatoes, vegetables, etc., same as an entree. Certainly can used with boiled rice too.

No. 18.—STEAKS CURRIED.

Same as chops curried, but to fry the steaks first, then proceed same as for mutton chops. Mashed potatoes should join this dish, and boiled spinach fried in butter with an onion will be a nice accompaniment, but tough part of beef wouldn't do neither. You must not beat up the steaks with a chopper or steak tenderer, because all the juice will be out; scarcely any taste. When serving add a few drops of lemon juice, and this Curry will taste nicer if gleeced before sending to table in the following way:— Set a stew-pan on fire, when hot put a small bit of butter and a small onion, finely sliced, and teaspoon of any gravy. Now use a wooden spoon for frying the onions, and press them in the sauce-pan. When nice and brown colour, and the fried onions have stuck in the sauce-pan, pour the Curry you prepared and a spoon of cream; let it simmer a few minutes. Send to table with rice. Don't forget to add lemon juice or vinegar.

No. 19.—GAME CURRIES (Various).

The Game Curry I mean is thus:—elk; venisons; poultry, as turkey, geese, duck, etc.; rabbit, etc. Can be curried same as No. 4, but it is not nicer to make them into a yellow Curry, as for fish or vegetables.

No. 20.—RABBIT OR YOUNG HARE CURRY.

N.B.—I think the Rabbit made into a gleeced brown stew much nicer than putting it in a jar, and prepare like a jugged hare, as it takes away all the flavour, and the gravy tastes nice, and the meat almost like the soup meat or plain boiled meat; but the Curried Rabbit is not a bad recipe, if properly made, to use as an ordinary entree.

Take a small rabbit; skin it; and cut up in small pieces as large as two inch square; flour it, and fry in butter or lard, just underdone, and brown it outside; keep it to a side. Now place a stew-pan on fire, and add the remaining butter or lard you fried the rabbit with; when this lard is nice and hot, slice one onion, and brown in the stew-pan. Now add Curry powder same as Madras Curry, No. 4. When all these are nice and brownish gold, add a pint of gravy or milk, and let it simmer gently on slow fire; and quarter of an hour before sending to table, add the fried rabbit to the Curry sauce, and let it simmer for 15 minutes. When serving add few drops of lemon juice, and a spoon of cream. The above Curry for boiled rice; if for an "entree," just cut the rabbit in joints, and prepare same as the above Curry. When serving add a glass of claret in place of lemon juice.

No. 21.—EGG CURRY (Whitish Yellow).

Hard boil six eggs, and put in cold water till wanted. Now place a stew-pan on fire, and add half teaspoon of saffron powder (yellow); half-pint of milk; one large onion, sliced; one tablespoon finely chopped ham or corned beef; one green capsicum, cut in quarters; one potato, mashed up (the potato left from last meal will do). Now simmer this for quarter of an hour; don't let it burn. When serving, take eggs out of the shell; cut in halves; place the eggs on a vegetable dish (the cut part up). Now add a tablespoon of cream, and a few drops of lemon juice; salt to taste, and pour over the eggs, and send to table with a brown Curry to accompany the rice (boiled). Samball and fried herring may be sent with these above Curries and rice. Poppadoms[7] and Bombay ducks will be a good accompaniment if could be procured.

No. 22.—EGG CURRY (Brown).

Boil the eggs same as No. 21, and put in cold water till wanted. Now prepare Curry sauce (brown) as No. 26, pour over the eggs cut in halves, as egg Curry (yellow). Egg Curries always called in Ceylon "a rest-house Curry," because in several rest-houses in Ceylon usually not many visitors pass that way, beside these rest-house keepers cannot get fresh beef, etc. They always have plenty of eggs, fowls, native vegetables, etc., but egg Curry only can be made quick. When a gentleman is going from one planting district to another, a box cooly or a horse-keeper (groom) runs in front to a certain place, by order of his master. When he gets into the rest-house, the rest-house keeper knows that a gentleman is coming. At once he will order to kill a chicken and grill it in Scotch form? and boil two eggs; when this is doing the kitchen mate[8] will squeeze half of a cocoanut, with little water mix some saffron, salt green chillie, Maldive fish, etc., now he boils this for five minutes. There is the breakfast ready! The bill of fare may be thus:—Grilled chicken; boiled pumpkin or beans, sometimes potatoes; boiled rice; egg Curry; samball; tea, coffee, or beer, etc. The

28

dinner might be similar to above with addition of soup. Sometimes the Curries are made from native vegetables, as there is plenty of nice and wholesome vegetables in Ceylon (I mean) besides the English vegetables. The rest-houses are in place of refreshment rooms and eating-houses are in England.

No. 23.—EGG CURRY (Omelet).

Make a savoury omelet with chopped ham, parsley, etc. When done, cut in one-inch squares, and pour over the Curry sauce, brown or yellow, as Nos. 21 and 22.

N.B.—The omelet should only be made just before serving, as it will get tough, etc. The Curry sauce may be made beforehand.

No. 24.—EGG CURRY (Poached).

Prepare Curry sauce, brown or yellow, as Nos. 26, 27. When serving just let the Curry sauce simmer gently. Now break the eggs carefully and put in the Curry sauce, each separately. Same as poaching eggs in a frying-pan. The pan must be a wide stew-pan. When dishing you must carefully take the yolks without breaking them and pour over the gravy, and send to table with boiled rice; and thin slices of ham should be handed round with this Curry and rice. Don't forget the samball for every Curry, as well as fried red herring.

No. 25.—FRIED EGGS FOR CURRIES.

Beat up the eggs same as for savoury omelet, but omit the sweet herbs, add chopped ham, salt, pepper, dash of flour, and pinch of cayenne, and fry in butter or lard (same as omelets, or in small cakes). Send to table with the Curry and rice in separate dish. The above dish (usually the native way) not used in gentlemen's houses, but I recommend it to be tried.

No. 26.—CURRY SAUCE (Brown, for Meat of any sort).

Place a stew-pan on fire, add a spoonful of butter; when melted add one onion, sliced; when half brownish colour add a tablespoon and a half of coriander powder, one of rice powder as No. 48, a saltspoon saffron, a pinch of cumin-seed powder. Now turn this well with a wooden spoon. When nicely fried, add the spices as said in the Curry No. 4, ginger and garlic chopped up fine. Now add a pint of good gravy or fresh milk, and let it simmer on slow fire till you find it reduced to a half-pint. Add salt to taste, and a little cayenne if preferred hot. Now this Curry Sauce is ready. This sauce can be heated up with any cold meats, as beef, mutton, pork, poultry, game, etc., etc., because the meat cooked beforehand cannot be cooked up in the above sauce, only warmed up. When preparing, the meat should only be added to the gravy about five to ten minutes before serving. The above recipe is only suitable for cold meats, fried livers, chops, steaks, etc., etc. The above is a brown Curry for parties, like the Curry stuffs; but for yellow Curry with less Curry stuffs, etc., see the accompanying recipe. But in Ceylon or in India always two Curries, etc., accompany the rice; especially in Ceylon a brown and yellow Curry, etc., accompanies the rice to table.

No. 27.—YELLOW CURRY SAUCE (for Vegetables, Fish, etc.).

Slice one onion, one large spoonful of chopped-up ham (fresh, best) or nice corned beef (cooked), one green capsicum cut in quarters, one small teaspoon of saffron powder, pinch of cayenne pepper if preferred hot Curry, half-pint of milk, salt to taste. Now put all these into a clean stew-pan and set on fire for twenty minutes or more, simmer gently, and let it reduce to half-pint. When serving add few drops of lemon juice and a large spoon of cream. The above Curry Sauce is very nice for fish and vegetables. If it is cooked up vegetable or fish, just add ten minutes before serving. If it is fresh vegetable or fish, to be cooked in the sauce from the beginning; see their separate headings. The above Curry only second to a moley made of fish or fowl.

No. 28.—CURRIED FOWL (a Joint).

- 1 good-sized Fowl and Curry Stuffs.

Everything same as for Madras Curry, but an extra spoon of coriander powder and spoonful of cocoanut scraped up fine (*i.e.*, in England I have seen and also used cocoanut scraped and preserved in tins by some firm in London). This cocoanut can add to all kinds of brown

Curries, as it gives flavour to Curry; but it is a new idea, not suitable or used in the East for a Curry. Dress the fowl as for boiling, and boil it for few minutes (under-done). Keep this to a side, but don't waste the broth. Now place a large stew-pan on fire (large enough to hold the fowl), slice one large onion and fry in the butter. When nicely brown take out the onions and put in the fowl, and fry it all sides nice and gold colour, take the fowl out of the pan. Now add all the Curry stuffs, spices, ginger, garlic, etc., etc., and the broth that the fowl has been boiled in, and a half-pint of milk and bay leaves. Let all these simmer till the Curry Sauce is reduced to a pint or little more. Now add the fowl and turn it occasionally; do not let it burn. When serving, add a few drops of lemon juice or vinegar (pickled), a spoonful of cream, salt to taste, and cayenne if preferred. Send to table on a flat dish large enough to carve the fowl, and leave enough gravy to go round the table; I mean not juicy, neither dry. The above should be treated as a joint. If any left can be warmed up in frying-pan, the fowl cut in pieces, and send to table with fried potatoes, garnished with nice green cabbage (boiled), or Brussels sprouts will do best. The above will do better on a Sunday for dinner, as thus:—

Not a bad dinner for a small party.

- Beef, mullagatawny, and rice.
- Curried fowls, and plenty of vegetables and potatoes.
- Some kind of pudding.

No. 29.—CHICKEN MOLEY.

FOR TWO YOUNG CHICKENS AND SOME GRAVY.

Cut up the chicken in joints, and boil all the bones, etc., for gravy. Place a stew-pan on fire, add the chicken-bone gravy, half-pint milk, one small spoon of butter, one eggspoon saffron powder, one tablespoon of chopped ham, small pinch of cayenne, one bay leaf, spices (bit of cinnamon, two cloves), salt to taste, one onion sliced. Let it boil (I mean simmer) for five minutes, then add the chicken, set on slow fire till the meat is tender. When serving, mix a dessertspoon of flour in two tablespoons of cream in a tea cup, then add this into the moley and stir well; let simmer for two or three minutes. When dishing, add a few drops of lemon juice or pickled vinegar. The above dish should be light-yellow colour, the gravy thick as cream. Mashed potatoes and fried bacon may garnish this dish, with red carrots, cut fine and pretty, and stuck in the mashed potatoes round the dish. The above entree should be served up on a small flat dish for a dinner, lunch, supper, etc.

No. 30.—FISH MOLEY.

FOR TWO POUNDS OF SALMON.

N.B.—The Fish Moley is almost like a Curry (*see* Fish Curry, Salmon, No. 31).

Cut the salmon nearly an inch thick, then cut it in two inches long, one inch wide, or little round pieces. Now mix in a stew-pan the following:—a pint of fish stock, white gravy, or milk, one small spoon of butter, one egg-spoon saffron powder, one dessertspoonful finely-chopped ham, pinch of cayenne, one bay leaf, spices (bit of cinnamon or cloves), one large onion sliced, salt to taste. Mix all the above into the stew-pan, and set on fire. When it simmers, add the fish and let it simmer gently until the fish is done. When serving, mash up a boiled potato in two tablespoons of cream. Pour to the moley, and add few drops of lemon juice, and send to table with boiled potatoes (mashed up and baked in an oven), in shape as a pudding. Suppose if you have any cold fish boiled the day before, just only mix up the sauce and let it simmer till wanted, and add the fish five or ten minutes before sending to table. Any fresh beef, cold beef, mutton, etc., can be made into moley, but the fresh beef ought to be tender part—the under cut of a sirloin will do nicely. It cannot be made from pork, because it will not taste as nice as chicken or fish.

No. 31.—FISH CURRY (Salmon).

The fish Curry is made several different ways in Ceylon and India, as brown or yellow Curry, but similar to fish moley, hard-boiled egg Curry, No. 22, and the potato Curry, No. 35; but you must add a spoonful of chopped ham or corned beef, and use lemon juice, not vinegar. The fish Curry (brown) can be made same as Madras Curry, No. 4. But proceed to make the Curry Sauce, No. 26, then add the fish. As soon as the fish is tender, the Curry is ready. Don't add any butter to fish Curries. The native cooks use the coriander, saffron, chillies, etc., without roasting them in the frying-pan.—See "Home-

34

made Curry Powder," No. 1, but grinding it without roasting.

No. 32.—FISH CURRY (Various).

- Salmon.
- Haddocks.
- Soles.
- Whiting.
- Codfish.
- Whitebait.
- Fresh Herrings.
- Lobsters.
- Crabs.
- Oysters.
- Prawns.
- Shrimps, etc.

The above Fish Curries can be made same as Salmon Curry, No. 31, egg Curry (yellow), fish moley, Madras Curry, No. 4, but great care must be taken not to be burned. The soles and whiting are not nice when curried, and the oysters should be used without the liquor. Prawns and shrimps are celebrated Curries if they are freshly caught and properly prepared. Tamarind used for Fish Curries (brown) are very nice—better than lime (lemon) juice or vinegar.

No. 33.—TINNED SARDINES (Curried).

FOR A SMALL TIN OF SARDINES OF ONE DOZEN.

Take the sardines, and take off the black part; just finely scrape; with a spoon place on a tin or plate, and make it warm in an oven. Now make a Curry sauce (brown), same as No. 26, but less milk or gravy. The Curry sauce must not be more than a small tea cup, nice and thick, if not thicker,—just mash up a boiled potato, and add to the sauce. Just before serving, take each sardine carefully and place in the Curry sauce you made; do not stir it; set on slow fire for five minutes. When serving take each carefully without breaking, arrange them nicely on a Curry or vegetable dish; pour over the gravy, and send to table with boiled rice or hot toast. Any tinned fish can be made same as the above, except Yarmouth bloaters, smoked fish, salt fish, mackerel, etc., etc. Tinned salmon makes a nice Curry. Afraid it will mash up and be like a gruel instead of lumps. The above Curry sauce will answer to several boiled fish—boiled the day before.

No. 34.—VEGETABLE CURRIES (Various).

With reference to above, the potato, knol khol, turnips, carrots, parsnips, vegetable marrow, cucumber, beans, etc., can be made same way as potato Curry, No. 35; but cabbage, spinach, turnip tops (young shoots), Brussels sprouts, can be made same way as potato Curry, with same ingredients, but the cabbage, Brussels sprouts, etc., take little more time to tenderly boil; therefore extra gravy, milk, butter, and extra spoon of ham or corned beef. Onions should be added for greens. The more good gravy you add the better the Curry. As far as I have seen, there is not many English vegetables can be Curried, but

36

in India and Ceylon there is numberless vegetables, greens, grasses, etc., can be Curried.

No. 35.—POTATO CURRY.

FOR ONE POUND OF GOOD POTATOES (PEELED).

Cut them in half-inch squares; put them into a clean stew-pan with an eggspoon of saffron; one large onion, sliced; one large spoon of chopped ham or corned beef (salt to taste); three parts of a pint of milk. Mix well together; put in a bay leaf; set on fire, and let it simmer till the potatoes are tender. If the three-quarters pint of milk is not sufficient to tender the potatoes, add some good gravy (stock), but not brown stock. When serving, add a quarter pint of milk and a dessertspoon or more of cream, and let it simmer. When simmering add a few drops of lemon juice, and send to table with boiled rice. But a Brown Curry must accompany the above Curry.

No. 36.—CABBAGE CURRY.

Take half of a small cabbage, and cut it with a sharp knife as big as you cutting a lettuce for a salad; wash it thoroughly clean; put into a stew-pan with a pint of gravy, and boil it till half done. Now take it off the fire; add an eggspoonful of saffron powder; two large spoons of chopped ham, etc.; a pinch of cayenne (if required hot); one large onion, sliced; salt to taste. Mix well; set on fire. More gravy or milk should be added, till the cabbage is soft as usual form.

No. 37.—BEAN CURRY.

FOR A POUND OF FRENCH BEANS.

Cut up the beans one inch long and prepare same as the cabbage Curry. The same ingredients will do and must accompany a meat Curry to table. These Curries may only be gleeced, if you please, or can serve plain, but the gleece gives a nice smell and good taste. Any Curry can be gleeced. If you wish to make Curry of broad beans, must take off the thicker skin and weigh a pound; but broad beans are not a useful bean for Curry, but only better as a vegetable by cooking it in a jar with butter and mint.—See Vegetables for Table, as No. 53.

No. 38.—ONION CURRY.

Same as potato Curry, No. 35. The large onions should be cut in quarters, and the small onions put in whole; but in India and Ceylon we have onions (I mean the button onions with red skin) which makes a delicious Curry.

No. 39.—DEVILLED CABIN BIS-CUITS.

- 1 Onion sliced.
- 1 Dessertspoon Butter.
- 2 Tablespoons of good Beef Gravy.
- 1 Eggspoon or less of Cayenne.
- Pinch of Pepper; Salt to taste.
- 1 Small Potato mashed up.

- 1 Dessertspoon of Worcester Sauce (Lea & Perrins).

Mode.—Slice the onions and fry in a stew-pan with the butter; when the onions turn to a gold colour add all other ingredients. During you preparing the above, soak six cabin biscuits in boiling water for two minutes, then take it out of the water and dish the biscuits, and pour over the devil gravy you prepared. Cover the biscuits with gravy and serve hot. The above dish is good for lunch, etc.

No. 40.—DEVILLED MEAT (Various).

Same ingredients as for biscuits, No. 39, but meat must be cut two inches long and added to the stew-pan soon as the onions are fried. Give it stirring for some while by turning the pieces of meat in it. By-the-bye, the fresh meat should be fried a little brown, because fresh meat devilled always tough unless the meat is undercut. Extra spoons of gravy should be added to devilled meats. Cuttings from cold joints are nice devilled; but fresh beef ought to be of tender part (as I said before, undercut). Fowl, duck, mutton, turkey, geese can be done in same way (I mean from joints roasted beforehand); but you must reduce or exceed the ingredients for the amount of weight. The quantities given for devilled biscuits are sufficient for 1 lb., or less of meat. Be careful not to burn.— See Devilled Biscuits.

No. 41.—MOLLAGOO TANNEY, AND NOT MULLIGATAWNY.

- 2 Good Quarts of Gravy of Mutton Beef or Chicken Soup.
- 2 Large Spoons of Coriander Powder.
- 1 Tablespoon of Rice Powder as No. 48, and Pinch of Pepper.
- 1 Pint of good Milk.
- 2 Large Onions, sliced.
- 1 Piece of Ginger.
- 1 Garlic, small one.
- ½ Teaspoon of Cumin Powder.
- Pinch of Saffron.
- 1 Dessertspoon Butter.

Mode.—The Curry stuffs you use for mollagoo tanney should be very fine. Take a large stew-pan and mix all the above together, only one onion (sliced), garlic and ginger chopped up fine. Let these simmer for ten minutes, now strain it through a muslin or gravy strainer. Now fry the other onion in the dessertspoon of butter in another stew-pan. When the onions are browned add the mollagoo tanney with a small bay leaf, and skim off the grease, and send to table in a soup tureen as a soup; but this should be used instead of soup, or the first dish for a lunch or breakfast or dinner, but I recommend for dinner in Europe. Cut lemon should be handed round with the above and plain boiled rice. Fried red herring wouldn't be a bad accompaniment. In India the mullagatawny is used generally once a week—say on a Sunday or Wednesday. The natives usually have this mullagatawny on Fridays after their caste. Some mullagatawny are made of plain Curry stuffs, tamarind, etc., not worth for Europeans. Some parties who visited India like native mullagatawny better than the above, according to taste, but I recommend the above for Europeans. The cayenne pepper should be added if required hot.

No. 42.—PILLAU RICE (a Mohammedan Dish), au Joint for Dinner.

Cook rice as No. 50. Keep it aside till wanted, then place a frying-pan on fire. Have two large onions (sliced) and two tablespoons of butter, and add half-teaspoon of saffron. When all the above is nicely brown add the rice, and keep on turning for few minutes, sprinkle a little salt. Now this is ready after dishing the above. Fry a large onion (sliced), and raisins (fried), sliced almonds. Sprinkle the above three over the pillau rice. The pillau rice should accompany roast fowl or mutton chops by dishing the meat on a flat dish, and cover it with pillau rice, and sprinkle over with fried onions, etc. Parsley mint can be fried and added. If it is to be eaten with Curry, use Madras Curry, kabob, or salmon, and omit the meat with pillau.

No. 43.—LEMON (HOT) SAUCE.

- Juice of a Large Lemon.
- 1 Dessertspoon Cayenne.
- 1 Dessertspoon Pounded White Sugar; some Salt.

Mix all together in a cup and use. If required to be kept, boil the whole in an enamel-plated saucepan; when cold bottle it. This sauce is very nice with cold meat or with made dishes.

No. 44.—APPLE CHUTNEY.

How to make in England.

- ½ lb. Sour Apples, peeled and cored.
- ¼ lb. Currants.
- 1 oz. Chillies (or ½ oz. Cayenne).
- 1 Tablespoon Brown Sugar.
- 4 oz. Salt, or to taste.
- 1 Eggspoon Pepper, finely ground.
- 1 oz. Garlic, chopped up fine.
- ¼ oz. Green Ginger, chopped up fine.
- ¼ lb. Raisins.

Mode.—Have the currants and raisins clean, and pound them in grinder or pounder of stone. Now grind the apples and all other ingredients to a smooth paste (I mean, not too thin or in lumps). Now mix these well together with half bottle of best vinegar, and bottle it in tart fruit bottles, corked well. If you require sweeter have more sugar, and if it is too watery put in a little less of vinegar. The above plan of chutney is suitable for cold meats, Curries, etc. In Ceylon, Mango Chutney is made in similar way, but they use tamarind, and when grinding use vinegar to soften the ingredients when grinding.

No. 44a.—MINT CHUTNEY.

- ½ lb. Mint.
- 1 oz. Cayenne.
- ¼ lb. Salt.
- ¼ lb. Raisins.
- 2 oz. Ginger.
- ¼ lb. Brown Sugar.
- 1 oz. Garlic.
- ½ Bottle Vinegar to grind the above.
- ½ Bottle Vinegar, hot, to pour over.

Mode.—Grind or pound the above by adding the cold vinegar by degrees to soften. When nice and smooth, put into a bowl and pour over the hot vinegar. When cool, bottle it in tart fruit bottles, and cork well.

N.B.—I can give dozens of recipes for chutney. I am afraid it is no use telling in this book, because the ingredients cannot be procured fresh, as mangoes, pineapples, lavi-lavi, blinga, tamarind, ripe chillies, chutnies, etc., etc. The above is a recipe I tried in Newera Eliya, Ceylon, where fresh mint can be had in any quantity of first class, same as in England and Scotland.

No. 45.—QUICKLY-MADE SAMBALL.

How to make it in England.

Chop up fine one large onion, a teaspoon of cayenne, another of crushed sugar, one tablespoon finely-chopped ham (cooked), one teaspoon salt, one tablespoon vinegar or lemon juice.

Mode.—Mix all the above in a small bowl with a wooden spoon or with your clean finger. Now add the vinegar. Again mix well, and send to table with cold pork, Curries, etc. A little more sugar may be added if preferred sweet. There are great many samballs can be made, but all must pass the Curry stone or stone-made pounder. The samballs made of dry chillies, green chillies, cocoanut juice, Maldive fish, onions, cooked fishes, meats, mint, etc., etc. The samballs are a great improvement to Curries. In Ceylon every cook would send a samball to table with the Curry and rice; also native meals are never without a samball—especially *samball*, or some ball. It is only a new-made chutney or pickle, but *fresh* made, called *sampball*.

No. 46.—HOW TO FRY RED HER-RINGS FOR CURRIES.

Take two stout common red herrings, cut them about one and a-half inch long (cross ways); put in a plate and add one tablespoon of vinegar and a little dash of cayenne; roll the herrings well, and fry them in butter or lard, and send to table dry, free from grease. To be eaten with rice and Curry instead of Bombay ducks.

The above is a new idea, which I came to know during my first visit to England, Royal Jubilee Exhibition, 1887, in Liverpool.

No. 47.—TOAST CURRY.

Prepare some Curry gravy, same as Madras Curry, No. 4. Now toast two slices of bread; cut thin, and in diamond shape. After toasted, dish the toast on a vegetable dish, and pour over the gravy you prepared, and send to table hot, with Curry and rice, samball, etc.

No. 48.—HOW TO MAKE RICE POW-DER.

Take a pound of good rice, and pick out all the black and other things from it. And now place a frying-pan on fire; soon as it gets hot put in the rice, and keep on turning till you find it nice and brown colour; then put on a plate to get cool; then pound this in a stone-made mortar or pounder (very fine), and bottle it, well corked. Use a tablespoon to brown Curries.

No. 49.—MUSHROOMS CURRIED AND SERVED ON TOAST.

Pick out half-pound of fresh and good mushrooms; sprinkle with little pepper and salt. Now prepare Curry sauce as for Snipe Curry. Fry the mushrooms in a dessertspoon of butter, and add to the Curry sauce; let it simmer gently for five minutes, then serve on hot toast. A nice dish for lunch or supper. When eating, a dash of cayenne and mushroom ketchup may be a nice taste. Try the above.

No. 50.—RICE, HOW TO BOIL FOR CURRIES.

Take an enamelled saucepan to hold four quarts, and fill it three-quarters full of fresh water, and let it boil.

During the time the water is boiling, soak two pounds of rice (white) for three minutes in cold water; then strain off the water, and put the rice in the pan that is boiling, and stir for two minutes, and cover it up. When boiling put in a spoon, and take out some rice and feel it with your finger. If it is done drain off all the water, and place the pan near a hot oven till wanted.

Must not let it be overdone. If it is overdone and nearly soft, just drain the boiling rice water, and add a few cups of very cold water. Stir it, and drain again, and set by the fire or on hot oven for a few minutes, and you will find each grain separate. Boiled rice ought to have each grain separate.

N.B.—The rice I have seen in England they call it "Patcha Areysi," used for rice cakes, etc., in India and Ceylon, etc. I mean the rice taken out the shell without boiling the paddy. The rice taken out the shell, called "Sothareysigal," as follows, of Rangoon, Chittagong, Bengal, etc., etc.:—

- Samba.
- Muthoo Samba.
- Mollagoo Samba.
- Oosi Samba.
- Collundha.
- Bangalam.
- Cara.
- Vallareysee.
- Masareysi.
- Waddakathy Samba.

And several other native names too numerous to mention. The above all good for eating after boiled.

No. 51.—A SALAD FOR DINNER, Etc., for Hot Weather.

- Cucumber.
- Beet Root, boiled.
- Hard-Boiled Eggs.
- Ripe Tomatoes.
- Water-Cress.
- 1 Large Onion, thin sliced.
- Cold Fowl, Beef, or Mutton.

Mode.—Cut the meat in thin slices, and put in a flat dish, then slice the cucumber, beet root, eggs, tomato, and onion, and dress the dish with the above, neatly arranging by putting one piece cucumber, another of beet root, another of eggs, and another of tomato, and put the sliced onions in the middle, and the water-cress round the dish as a decoration. Now prepare this

SAUCE.

- Yolks of 2 Hard Boiled Eggs.
- 1 Potato, finely mashed up.
- 1 Dessertspoon of Made Mustard.
- 1 Teaspoonful of crushed Sugar, another of Butter.
- 2 Dessertspoons of Condensed Milk (omit the Sugar); or,
- 1 Large spoon of Cream instead of Condensed Milk.
- ½ Teaspoon of Salt, Dash of Cayenne and Pepper.
- 3 Tablespoons Vinegar, or more.

Take a small bowl and mash up the potato, yolks of eggs, mustard, sugar, salt, butter. When nice and smooth add the milk or cream. After mixed add the vinegar, and mix well and keep separate. When sending to table just pour the sauce all over the salad with a spoon. Let it stand for two minutes and serve. The above can be made with or without meat, and also with lettuce if at hand. Several other salads could be made as learned cooks have written in the cooks' books; but the above I tried myself in one of my former masters' bungalows in Ceylon and in England.

No. 52.—SUNDAL OR POOGATHU (a Native Dish).

Finely cut one cabbage (a small one)—I mean as fine as the tobacco used for cigarettes, put a stew-pan on fire, add a small spoonful of butter, one onion (sliced). When the onions are nice and brown put in the cabbage, give it a turn, and add a teacup of good gravy, and cover it up, and set on gentle fire for few minutes; then add a spoonful of chopped ham, dash of cayenne and pepper, a pinch of saffron powder, and set over an oven till wanted. Do not let it burn; keep on turning. When nice and dry send to table with Curry, and rice, and samball. The above can be made from any greens; but this is not in use in European houses in Ceylon, but very nice dish for Curries.

No. 53.—VEGETABLES BOILED FOR TABLE.

French beans, broad beans, peas, Brussels sprouts, etc., will be nice when boiled in preserve jar with a lump of butter, salt, and dash of pepper (and mint to peas), but Brussels sprouts requiring lots of cooking may add some water to it. Spinach and sorrel can be cooked in a jar with a small onion (sliced), and little more salt to sorrel. Any vegetables might be done as above. I think it is an economical way of cooking vegetables; but I am afraid it wouldn't do for large establishments as hotels, etc., but for family houses it is a better way. The jar to be placed in a large pan, half full of water, and see it occasionally to prevent drying up.

No. 54.—ECONOMICAL CURRY PASTE.

- 1 lb. Coriander Seed.
- ¼ lb. Dry Chillies.
- ½ lb. Mustard Seed.
- 2 oz. Garlic.
- 2 oz. ——
- ½ lb. Dried Peas.
- ½ pint Vinegar.
- ¼ lb. Saffron.
- ¼ lb. Pepper.
- 2 oz. Dry Ginger.
- ½ lb. Salt.
- ½ lb. Brown Sugar.
- 2 oz. Cumin Seed.

- ½ pint Lucca Oil.

N.B.—Few Bay Leaves in Ceylon and India. Using Carugapilbay or *Curry Leaves*, black.

Mode.—Grind all the above with the vinegar using to moisten the ingredients, using a Curry stone or stone-made pounder. When all the above nice and thin as a paste, put in a jar and pour over the Lucca oil, and cover it up. Use a large spoon for Madras Curries. The above good for mushroom, snipe, partridge, and other brown Curries of superior quality.

No. 55.—CURRY POWDER (a Recipe).

- 2 lbs. Coriander Seed.
- ½ oz. Chillies.
- 4 oz. Pepper.
- 7 oz. Cumin Seed.
- 7 oz. Mustard Seed.
- 1 oz. Bay Leaves.
- 8 oz. Carum Seed.
- 2 oz. Saffron.

Make all the above into powder, and calculate the weight—ought to equal. Use one and a-half tablespoonful for brown Curries only.

No. 56.—CURRY POWDER (a Recipe).

- 1 lb. Coriander Seed.

- ¼ lb. Cumin Seed.
- 6 oz. Saffron.
- 10 oz. Dry Chillies.
- 2½ oz. Vantheyam (Tamil name) Fenugreek.
- 4 oz. Ginger.
- 1 Handful chopped-up Bay Leaves.

Pound smooth all these, and bottle it in, well corked, and use as above. The above three recipes are from Mr. Symon Nayajam, cook, of Madras and Colombo, Ceylon.

No. 57.—CURRY POWDER (a most excellent).

- 2 Large Old Fowls.
- 1 lb. Coriander.
- ⅛ lb. Chillies or Cayenne.
- 6 oz. Saffron.
- 2 Large Spoons Cumin Seed.
- 1 oz. Dry Ginger.
- 2 oz. Garlic.
- 4 Large Spoons of Rice Powder, as No. 48; or 4 Large Spoons of Dried Peas (roasted and ground).
- ½ Handful Dried Bay Leaves.
- 1 Tablespoon Peppercorns.
- 2 doz. Cloves.
- ¼ lb. Button Onions,
- ¼ lb. Butter or Ghee.

Mode.—Clean the fowls and cut them in small pieces, the giblets and all. Put into a large saucepan, and add a few quarts of water, and boil it very tender—I mean simmer gently for two days. The bones, meat, etc., should be mashed up. Now take out all the bones, and keep to a side. Take a large saucepan, put in the butter and sliced onions, and fry it to a brown colour. Now add all the Curry Powders, garlic chopped up, bay leaves, dry ginger, cloves, pepper, all in powders, and fry gently for a few minutes. Now add the gravy of boiled fowls, with the meat, etc., and let it simmer so a few minutes. When all these are reduced to three quarts, just dish it on a flat dish and let it cool for a day, or till it gets hard as a brick. Now pound this in a stone-made mortar to a smooth powder, and bottle it, well corked, and use for Brown Curries, a dessertspoon to a pound, with sliced onions, milk or gravy, and lemon juice.

N.B.—The above recipe is a most excellent of all the Curry Powders and Pastes, only second to none. In India we can prepare the above with tamarind included, for acid taste, and few other ingredients which can get fresh in Ceylon and India, but I think not procurable in England.

No. 58.—TOMATO CURRY.

For a pound of young or green tomato, ingredients same as for Potato Curry, No. 35, or for Brown Curry same as No. 4, Madras Curry. Treat it same as the Cabbage Curry. But I recommend that tomatoes should be made Brown Curry—tastes nice. Tomato curried is better than all the vegetables if it is properly made. Ripe tomato not nice when curried, only for salads.

No. 59.—CURRIES UNDER VARIOUS NAMES.

As to my opinion, Curries can be made from anything, if you could procure the proper Curry Powders, etc. Almost every Curry is made one or two ways, by only reducing, exceeding, or mixing the various Curry stuffs. Some Curries are hot, some dry, some juicy, some sour, and so on. Then the cooks celebrate the names in the menu as Delhi Curry, Agra Curry, Madras Curry, Curry à la Punjab, Bengal Curry, Mysore Curry, and several other names too numerous to mention in this little work. But I myself and several parties who have visited India will be glad to recommend Madras Curries as best; and Ceylon Singhalese Curry (yellow) is good, made of cocoanut juice, Maldive fish, lemon, Curry leaves, saffron, etc. Several cooks add too much ghee or butter, lard, etc., but it only spoils the taste of the Curry; and some cooks put too much spice, and give it too much flavouring. Reasonable ingredients couldn't spoil a Curry. A small girl of 10 years of age will make a Curry, as Curries are easily made in India and Ceylon.

No. 60.—CHUTNEY CHICKEN.

Same as country capon, or country captian, but mix few tablespoons of mango chutney, or any other chutneys, but not hot.

No. 61.—WHEN TO USE CURRIES.

First Course.

- Soup.
- Fish.
- Entrees.
- Joints.

Second Course.

- Curry and Rice.
- Sweets.
- Cheese.
- Dessert.
- Coffee.

TAMIL AND ENGLISH NAMES FOR CURRY STUFFS, etc., as used in Ceylon.

I only give a few of Tamil languages as generally in use, but not high words. Many parties visited our Indian continent will understand the following and names of native vegetables:—

ENGLISH.	TAMIL.
Rice.	Areysi.
Curry.	Currie.
Coriander.	Cotha Mulle.
Saffron.	Münjal.
Cumin Seed.	Seeragam.
Ginger, Dry.	Sukkoo.
Ginger, Green.	Engi.
Salt.	Oopoo.
Dry Chillie.	Cotchi Kaie.
Green Chillie.	Patcha Kotchi Kaie.
Cocoanut.	Thankaie or Thayangaie.
Maldive Fish.	Massi.
Milk.	Paal.
Bread.	Rotti.
Sugar.	Sèèney.
Water.	Thannir.
Cocoanut Oil.	Thankaie Annay.

Ghee.	Naie.
Butter.	Vannai.
Onions.	Vengayam.
Curry Leaves.	Caruga Pillay.
Lemon or Limes.	Thascekaie.
Tamarind.	Puley.
Cinnamon.	Carova Patta.
Cloves.	Ikramba.
Dry Fish.	Caroowadoo.
Fish.	Meen.
Beef.	Erratchi.
Mutton.	Art Erratchi.
Pork.	Pandi Erratchi.
Fowl.	Coley.
Chicken.	Coley Kunju.

ARTICLES OF FOOD—POSANA PATHARITLAUGAL.

Meat.	Ereitchi.
Fresh Meat.	Patcha Eratchi.
Ghie Fish.	Ney Meen.
Soles.	Nakoo Meen.
Shrimps.	Cooni, Erraal.
Prawn.	Erraal.
Lobster.	Singeerral.
Crab.	Nandoo.
Turkey.	Van Coley.
Goose.	Peria Vathu, or Wathu.

Teal.	Seeragi.
Snipe.	Collan or Collaan.

CEREALS.	THANIYA VAGAYI.
Boiled Rice.	Soru.
Pearl Barley.	Barli Arisi.
Sago.	Sav-vari-si.
Kurrakan Raggy.	Koorakan *Kapay*.
Maize.	Sollam, Mākka, Solam.
Pulses.	Payaroo Vagaie.
Grain.	Kadalay, Thaniam.
Flour.	Mahà, Vagai.
Wheat Flour.	Gothuma Mā.
Corn Flour.	Sollam Mā.
Tapioca.	Eli lay Mā.
Arrowroot.	Coova Mā.
Cabbage.	Govis Keeray.
Cucumber.	*Wellari*.
Pumpkin.	Poosani Kai.
Bringall.	Kathari Kay.
Wenda Kay.	Wenda Kai.
Drumstick.	Mooroonga Kai.
Curry Stuffs.	Masalai.
Pepper.	Melagu.
Mustard.	Kadoogoo.
Garlic.	Vella Vengāyam.
Fenugreek.	Vanthayam.

Dark Margosa Leaves.	Caroova Pillay.
Aniseed.	Sōōmboo.
Cardamom.	Alāmor elam.
Nutmeg.	Sathi Kai.
Mace.	Sathi Pathari.
Lime.	Ellumitchan *Palam.*
Fruit.	Pala, Vagai.
Mango.	Mām *Palam.*
Plantain.	*Vala* Palam.
Custard Apple.	Seitha *Palam.*
Jack Fruit.	Paala, Palam.
Bread Fruit.	Lera Palla Kai.
Bullock's Heel.	Rama Seitha Palam.
Pine Apple.	Annāsi Palam.
Orange.	Pani Thottam, Palam.
Guava.	Coiya Palam.

I can give several other names in Tamil and English, but my little book is too light to carry the burden.

D. SANTIAGOE.